FIRST CODING

DATA AND MEMORY

By Sam Thompson

Gareth Stevens
PUBLISHING

Please visit our website, www.garethstevens.com. For a free color catalog of all our high-quality books, call toll free 1-800-542-2595 or fax 1-877-542-2596.

Cataloging-in-Publication Data
Names: Thompson, Sam.
Title: Data and memory / Sam Thompson.
Description: New York : Gareth Stevens, 2022. | Series: First coding | Includes glossary and index.
Identifiers: ISBN 9781538274354 (pbk.) | ISBN 9781538274378 (library bound) | ISBN 9781538274361 (6 pack) | ISBN 9781538274385 (ebook)
Subjects: LCSH: Computer storage devices–Juvenile literature. | Computer programming–Juvenile literature.
Classification: LCC TK7895.M4 T466 2022 | DDC 004.5–dc23

This edition is published by arrangement with Booklife Publishing

Published in 2022 by
Gareth Stevens Publishing
29 E. 21st Street
New York, NY 10010

Written by: Sam Thompson
Edited by: Madeline Tyler
Designed by: Dan Scase

Printed in the United States of America

CPSIA compliance information: Batch #CWGS22: For further information contact Gareth Stevens, New York, New York at 1-800-542-2595.

Find us on

Photo credits

All images are courtesy of Shutterstock.com. With thanks to Getty Images, Thinkstock Photo and iStockphoto. Front cover – Prostock-studio, – RoryDesign, the_same_space, Lineicons freebird, Happy Art, RaulAlmu, airdone. 4&5 – myboys.me, AlesiaKan. 6&7 – Mauro Rodrigues, dourleak. 8&9 – Rawpixel.com, Wachiwit, Dmytro Khlystun, panuwat phimpha. 10&11 – Hitra, palidachan. 12&13 – PixieMe, sasirin pamai, Fireofheart. 14&15 – BEST-BACKGROUNDS, AlesiaKan. 16&17 – Iakov Filimonov, BEST-BACKGROUNDS. 18&19 – Castleski, Vadim Sadovski. 20&21 – NASA, Denise Panyik-Dale, Berkah Icon. 22&23 – Claudio Divizia, Tarzhanova, Rawpixel.com, Guitarfoto studio. Background on all pages – magic pictures. Tablet – Olga Lebedeva. Icons – RoryDesign, the_same_space, Lineicons freebird, Happy Art, RaulAlmu.

CONTENTS

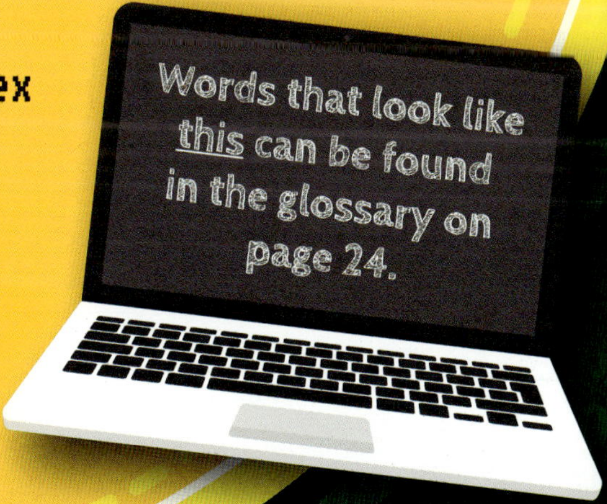

Words that look like <u>this</u> can be found in the glossary on page 24.

WHAT IS CODING?

Coding means telling a computer what to do by writing a set of instructions. The set of instructions is called a code. We use coding to do all sorts of amazing things on a computer.

Another word for coding is programming.

A computer is a machine that can follow instructions and store information.

Information is the numbers and facts that tell you about something.

Someone who writes code is called a programmer.

Bits of information are put together to make a program. The program is then run on a computer.

WHAT IS MEMORY?

Memory is any device that holds information and programs for a computer. For example, a hard drive is a fixed part of a computer's memory.

There are different types of memory. RAM is a type of memory that stores information for a very short amount of time.

This is an extra hard drive. Extra memory like this can help store even more information.

BITS AND BYTES

Information on a computer is stored as a file. A file might be a picture, a video, or a piece of information that helps a program run.

Files can be different sizes. Big files take up more memory, and small files take up less.

The size of a file is measured in bits and bytes. There are eight bits in a byte.

Around 1,000 bytes is a kilobyte. A simple text file can be around ten kilobytes.

Around 1 million bytes is a megabyte. A big picture can be one to five megabytes.

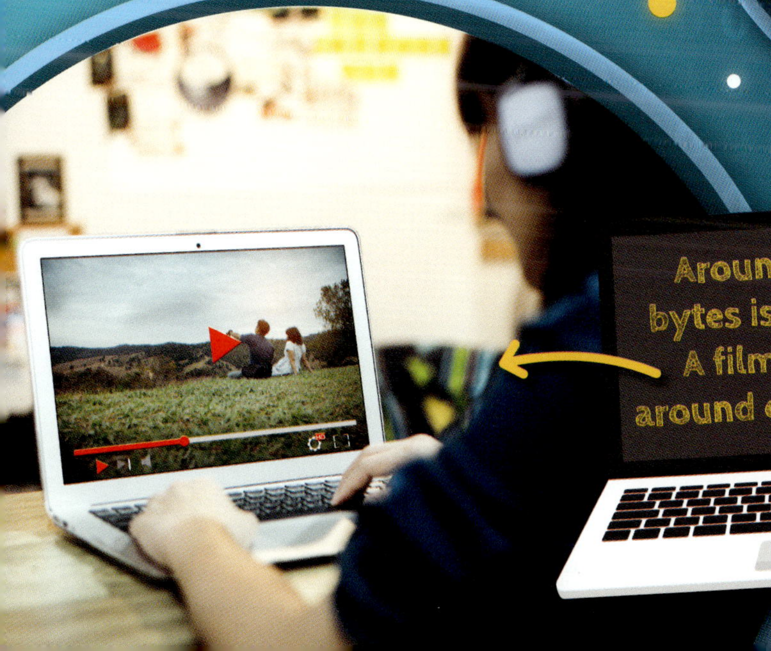

Around 1 billion bytes is a gigabyte. A film might be around one gigabyte.

DATA

Bits of information are called data. A school might have data about its pupils, such as names, ages, and where they live.

A database is a place to store data. Here the data can be ordered so it is easier to search through and find what you are looking for.

Hospitals use databases to keep track of data about the people they are caring for.

HOW TO USE A DATABASE

Many databases are made up of columns and rows. The columns go up and down, while the rows go across.

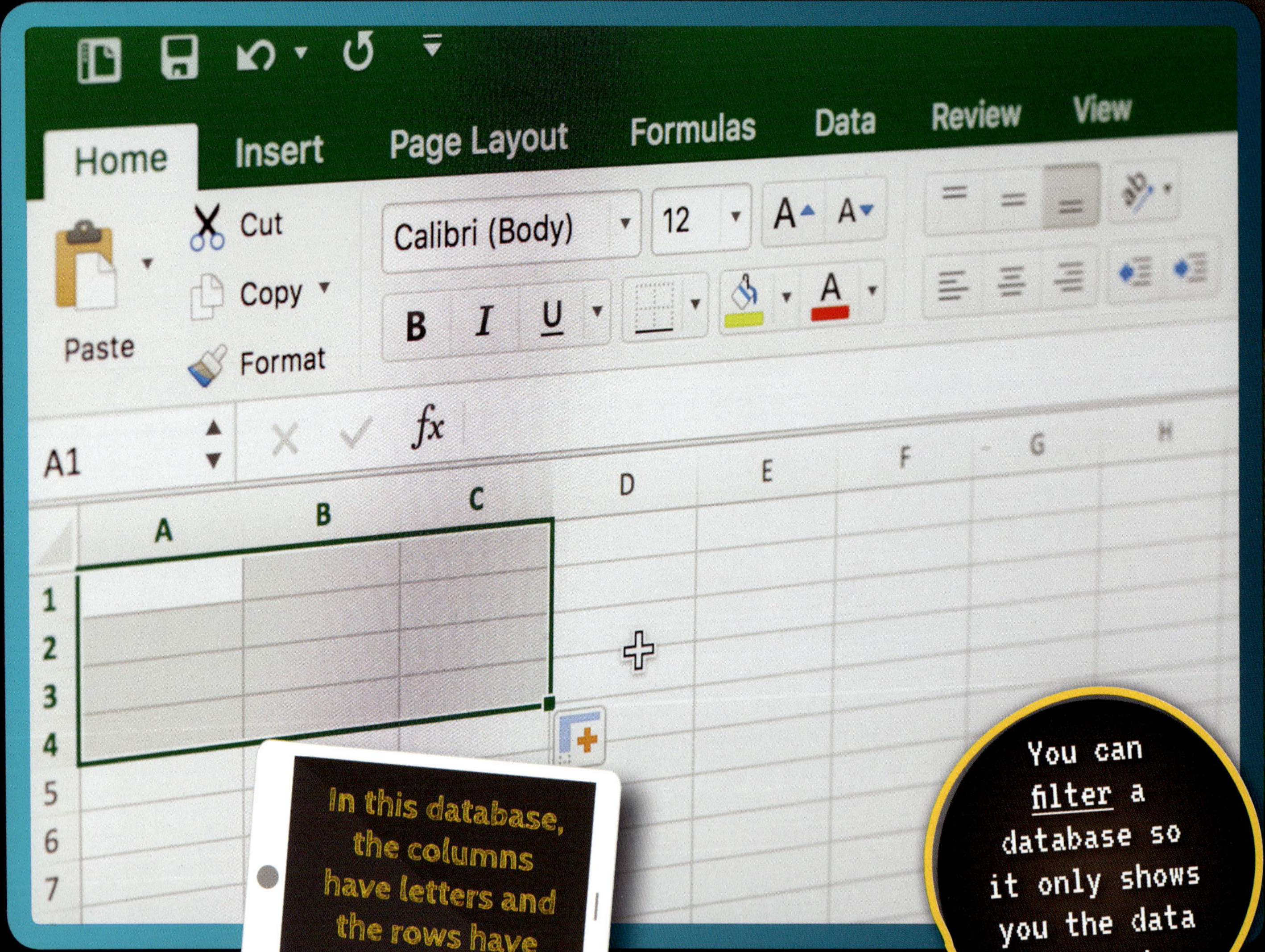

In this database, the columns have letters and the rows have numbers.

You can **filter** a database so it only shows you the data you want.

Columns tell you about the type of information. In a school database, there might be a column for a student's age or their favorite color. Rows are for things or people. There might be a row for each student.

NAME	AGE	FAVORITE COLOR	NUMBER OF SICK DAYS
Sally Comet	5	Gold	1
Ewan Cousin	4	Red	9
Kamal Allen	6	Blue	3
Les Barkman	6	Pink	4

VARIABLES

In programming, a variable is something that holds a piece of information. For example, a programmer might write:

```
age = 5
```

This means that "age" is a variable, and the information it holds is "5."

When writing a program, variables help computers remember information. If the computer is asked what "age" is, it knows "5" is the answer.

Variables are set up by the programmer.

CHANGING VARIABLES

The information that a variable holds can be changed. This can be very useful. Variables let programs interact with people and store new information.

Interacting means passing information between two things, or two things having an effect on each other.

For example, a programmer could tell the computer that the variable "age" will be whatever a person types in. Now the variable can change, and the age will be different depending on what the computer is told.

WHAT CAN CODING DO?

Amazing things can be done with coding. Lots of coding is involved with sending people into space. For example, coding creates the flight software that spacecraft use.

Coding helped send people to the moon.

Humans send machines called satellites into space. Satellites travel around Earth. They help us do all sorts of things, such as talk with smartphones and use satnavs.

FAMOUS PROGRAMMERS

ANNIE EASLEY

Computer Scientist

Annie Easley programmed code for NASA. Her work was very important in helping people travel in space. For example, her code was used to make better rockets. She also encouraged younger people to get into coding.

DENNIS RITCHIE

Computer Programmer

Dennis Ritchie built a programming language called C. Almost everything on the internet has been created using C or programming languages that exist because of C. Many apps use programming languages that need C too.

TIMELINE OF DATA

Punch cards were one of the first ways to store data. Each punch card stored around 80 bytes.

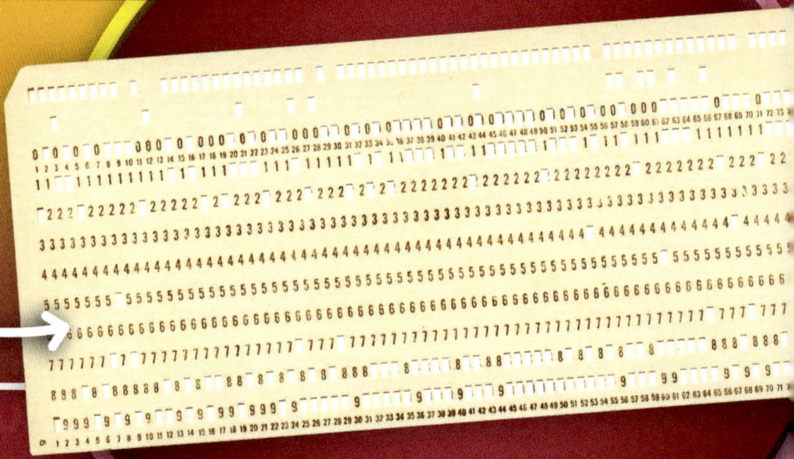

Today's smartphones are more powerful than the computers that sent the first people to the moon.

Floppy disks were used from around the 1970s to the 1990s. The first floppy disks stored around 80 kilobytes.

Many computers today use SSDs. Some SSDs can store up to one terabyte of memory. One terabyte is 1 trillion bytes.

Cloud storage is also used today. Cloud storage is when data is backed up on faraway servers and is able to be used over the internet. There is an almost never-ending amount of space!

Lots of data is created every year. In 2025, it is thought that 175 zettabytes of data will be created. A zettabyte could hold 36,000 years of video, or 250 billion DVDs.

GLOSSARY

device	a machine or invention made to do something
filter	remove unwanted things, making searching easier
flight software	technology used to help control a flying vehicle
instructions	a set of steps that explain how something is done
NASA	the U.S. space agency
programming language	a language that humans use to write instructions for computers
run	when a computer reads through all the instructions and does what it is told